W9-DEC-780

THE FALL OF THE CITY

by ARCHIBALD MAC LEISH

THE HAPPY MARRIAGE

THE POT OF EARTH

NOBODADDY (A PLAY)

STREETS IN THE MOON

THE HAMLET OF A. MAC LEISH

NEW FOUND LAND

CONQUISTADOR

FRESCOES FOR MR. ROCKEFELLER'S CITY

UNION PACIFIC—A BALLET

PANIC (A PLAY)

PUBLIC SPEECH: POEMS

THE FALL OF THE CITY (A VERSE PLAY FOR RADIO)

The
Fall of the City

A Verse Play for Radio

BY

ARCHIBALD MacLEISH

FARRAR & RINEHART, INC.

New York   *Toronto*

COPYRIGHT, 1937, BY ARCHIBALD MAC LEISH
PRINTED IN THE UNITED STATES OF AMERICA
BY QUINN & BODEN COMPANY, INC., RAHWAY, N. J.

For

A. B. L. and R. A. L.

The first performance over the air occurred Sunday Evening, April 11, 1937, from 7 to 7:30 Eastern Standard Time, over the Columbia Broadcasting System Network.

Production under the direction of Irving Reis, director of the Columbia Workshop.

CAST OF CHARACTERS

VOICE OF STUDIO DIRECTOR . .	*House Jamison*
VOICE OF ANNOUNCER . . .	*Orson Welles*
VOICE OF DEAD WOMAN . . .	*Adelaide Klein*
VOICE OF 1ST MESSENGER . . .	*Carlton Young*
VOICE OF ORATOR	*Burgess Meredith*
VOICE OF 2ND MESSENGER . .	*Dwight Weist*
VOICE OF PRIEST	*Edgar Stehli*
VOICE OF GENERAL	*William Pringle*
VOICES OF ANTIPHONAL CHORUS	*Guy Repp* *Brandon Peters* *Karl Swenson* *Dan Davies* *Kenneth Delmar*

Citizens, dancers, priests, soldiers, etc.

FOREWORD

ANY introduction is a confession of weakness. This one is no exception. It is written because I am anxious to persuade American poets to experiment with verse plays for radio and because I am quite certain the radio verse play I have written will not persuade them of itself.

The argument for radio as a stage for verse is neither long nor sensational. It consists largely in asserting what everyone knows. But such is the character of what everyone knows that no one knows it with enthusiasm. On the basis of the most obvious and elementary facts every poet with a dramatic leaning—and what poet ever lived who was really satisfied with writing the thin little books to lie on the front parlor tables?—should have been storming the studios for years. And yet actually the storming has been thin and infrequent. The British Broadcasting Corporation has presented a few verse plays written expressly for radio and one of them, Geoffrey Bridson's *March of the '45*, is said to have been both interesting and exciting. But the American slate is still approximately clean.

The first fact which everyone knows is that radio is a mechanism which carries to an audience sounds and nothing but sounds. A radio play consists of words and word equivalents and nothing else. There is no visible actor disguised to assume a part. There is no stage-set contrived to resemble a

[ix]

place. There is only the spoken word—an implement which poets have always claimed to use with a special authority. There is only the word-excited imagination—a theater in which poets have always claimed peculiar rights to play. Nothing exists save as the word creates it. The word dresses the stage. The word brings on the actors. The word supplies their look, their clothes, their gestures. The more packed and allusive the word, the more illuminating its rhythms, the more perfectly is the scene prepared, the more convincingly is the play enacted. On the stage, verse is often an obstacle because the artifice of the verse and the physical reality of the scene do not harmonize: it is for this reason that verse is easily accepted on the stage only where the scene is made remote in time and therefore artificial to begin with, or where the verse is blurred out and made to sound as much as possible like prose. But over the radio verse is not an obstacle. Over the radio verse has no visual presence to compete with. Only the ear is engaged and the ear is already half poet. It believes at once: creates and believes. It is the eye which is the realist. It is the eye which must fit everything together, must see everything before and behind. It is the eye and not the ear which refuses to believe in the lovely girlhood of the middle-aged soprano who sings Isolde, or the delicate, water-troubling slenderness of the three fat Rhine maidens ridiculously paddling at the ends of three steel ropes. With the eye closed or staring at nothing verse has every power over the ear. The ear accepts, accepts and believes, accepts and creates. The ear is the poet's perfect audience, his only true audience. And it is radio and only radio which can give him public access to this perfect friend.

[x]

The second fact which everyone knows and no one observes is the fact that the technique of radio, the ordinary, commercial technique, has developed tools which could not have been more perfectly adapted to the poet's uses had he devised them himself. Writers of prose plays for radio have practically unanimously ignored these tools. They have written for radio precisely as they would write for stage and many, if not most, radio plays have been nothing but stage plays adapted to the microphone. The tools nevertheless exist and the chief of them is the Announcer. The Announcer is the most useful dramatic personage since the Greek Chorus. For years modern poets writing for the stage have felt the necessity of contriving some sort of chorus, some sort of commentator. There is no occasion here to go into the reasons: they are compelling enough. But this chorus, this commentator, has always presented an extremely awkward practical problem. How justify its existence dramatically? How get it on? How get it off again? In radio this difficulty is removed before it occurs. The commentator is an integral part of radio technique. His presence is as natural as it is familiar. And his presence, without more, restores to the poet that obliquity, that perspective, that three-dimensional depth without which great poetic drama cannot exist.

These two facts alone ought to be persuasive enough. But there are more. There are practical reasons. With the suspension of the experimental work of the Federal Theatre Units which presented such important plays as *Murder in the Cathedral* and Auden's *Dance of Death,* there no longer exists a theater in New York in which a man interested in carrying modern poetry to the stage can be assured of a hearing. The

[xi]

Guild no longer has experimental interests. The Group is temporarily suspended. And the consequence is that any man who proposes to attack the problem must present himself to the commercial producers—who quite properly have their own ideas of what verse on Broadway ought to be. The producers are not to blame for a natural reluctance to back experimental verse plays. They are not in business to experiment. And the costs they are obliged to meet are exceedingly high. But the fact of their reluctance is an additional reason for turning to radio. For in radio the costs of production are relatively low and the material obstacles correspondingly reduced. Some of the most competent readers of verse to be heard in this country—Mr. Orson Welles and Mr. Burgess Meredith for example —are available from time to time in the broadcasting studios. Music, and the like, is readily arranged. And the extra costs of presenting a verse play are, in consequence, modest enough. Furthermore the studios, unlike the theatrical producers, are not apt to think of themselves as performing deeds of aesthetic charity whenever they produce serious works of art. Their own need of good material is too notorious.

Over and above all this there is the great question of audience. No man who has had the experience of presenting plays first before Broadway audiences and thereafter before such audiences as the radical theaters provide would ever of his own choice return to the Broadway audience. Radio will not of course provide the immediate sense of the live and vigorous audience which the radical theaters give. But radio will reach an infinitely greater number of people and should be capable, in time and with adequate materials, of shaping sections of that greater number into a living audience which

the poet and his actors can feel. This consideration alone
should deeply move the American poet whose present tragedy
is his isolation from any audience vigorous enough to demand
his strongest work.

A. MacL.

Farmington, Connecticut,
December, 1936.

THE FALL OF THE CITY

THE FALL OF THE CITY

VOICE OF THE STUDIO DIRECTOR (*orotund and professional*)

Ladies and gentlemen:
This broadcast comes to you from the city
Listeners over the curving air have heard
From furthest-off frontiers of foreign hours—
Mountain Time: Ocean Time: of the islands:
Of waters after the islands—some of them waking
Where noon here is the night there: some
Where noon is the first few stars they see or the last one.

For three days the world has watched this city—
Not for the common occasions of brutal crime
Or the usual violence of one sort or another
Or coronations of kings or popular festivals:
No: for stranger and disturbing reasons—
The resurrection from death and the tomb of a dead woman.

Each day for three days there has come
To the door of her tomb at noon a woman buried!

The terror that stands at the shoulder of our time
Touches the cheek with this: the flesh winces.
There have been other omens in other cities
But never of this sort and never so credible.

[3]

In a time like ours seemings and portents signify.
Ours is a generation when dogs howl and the
Skin crawls on the skull with its beast's foreboding.
All men now alive with us have feared.
We have smelled the wind in the street that changes weather.
We have seen the familiar room grow unfamiliar:
The order of numbers alter: the expectation
Cheat the expectant eye. The appearance defaults with us.

Here in this city the wall of the time cracks.

We take you now to the great square of this city. . . .

*(The shuffle and hum of a vast patient crowd
gradually rises: swells: fills the background.)*

VOICE OF THE ANNOUNCER (*matter-of-fact*)

We are here on the central plaza.
We are well off to the eastward edge.
There is a kind of terrace over the crowd here.
It is precisely four minutes to twelve.
The crowd is enormous: there might be ten thousand:
There might be more: the whole square is faces.
Opposite over the roofs are the mountains.
It is quite clear: there are birds circling.
We think they are kites by the look: they are very high. . . .

The tomb is off to the right somewhere—
We can't see for the great crowd.
Close to us here are the cabinet ministers:
They stand on a raised platform with awnings.

[4]

The farmers' wives are squatting on the stones:
Their children have fallen asleep on their shoulders.
The heat is harsh: the light dazzles like metal.
It dazes the air as the clang of a gong does. . . .

News travels in this nation:
There are people here from away off—
Horse-raisers out of the country with brooks in it:
Herders of cattle from up where the snow stays—
The kind that cook for themselves mostly:
They look at the girls with their eyes hard
And a hard grin and their teeth showing. . . .

It is one minute to twelve now:
There is still no sign: they are still waiting:
No one doubts that she will come:
No one doubts that she will speak too:
Three times she has not spoken.

    (The murmur of the crowd changes—
    not louder but more intense: higher.)

    THE VOICE OF THE ANNOUNCER *(low but with increasing*
      excitement)

Now it is twelve: now they are rising:
Now the whole plaza is rising:
Fathers are lifting their small children:
The plumed fans on the platform are motionless. . . .

There is no sound but the shuffle of shoe leather . . .

Now even the shoes are still. . . .

We can hear the hawks: it is quiet as that now. . . .

It is strange to see such throngs so silent. . . .

Nothing yet: nothing has happened. . . .

Wait! There's a stir here to the right of us:
They're turning their heads: the crowd turns:
The cabinet ministers lean from their balcony:
There's no sound: only the turning. . . .

(*A woman's voice comes over the silence of
the crowd: it is a weak voice but penetrating:
it speaks slowly and as though with difficulty.*)

THE VOICE OF THE DEAD WOMAN

First the waters rose with no wind. . . .

THE VOICE OF THE ANNOUNCER (*whispering*)

Listen: that is she! She's speaking!

THE VOICE OF THE DEAD WOMAN

Then the stones of the temple kindled
Without flame or tinder of maize-leaves. . . .

THE VOICE OF THE ANNOUNCER (*whispering*)

They see her beyond us: the crowd sees her. . . .

[6]

THE VOICE OF THE DEAD WOMAN

Then there were cries in the night haze:
Words in a once-heard tongue: the air
Rustling above us as at dawn with herons.

Now it is I who must bring fear:
I who am four days dead: the tears
Still unshed for me—all of them: I
For whom a child still calls at nightfall.

Death is young in me to fear!
My dress is kept still in the press in my bedchamber:
No one has broken the dish of the dead woman.

Nevertheless I must speak painfully:
I am to stand here in the sun and speak:

    (There is a pause. Then her voice comes
    again loud, mechanical, speaking as by rote.)

The city of masterless men
Will take a master.
There will be shouting then:
Blood after!

    (The crowd stirs. Her voice goes
    on weak and slow as before.)

Do not ask what it means: I do not know:
Only sorrow and no hope for it.

THE VOICE OF THE ANNOUNCER

She has gone. . . . No, they are still looking.

THE VOICE OF THE DEAD WOMAN

It is hard to return from the time past. I have come
In the dream we must learn to dream where the crumbling of
Time like the ash from a burnt string has
Stopped for me. For you the thread still burns:
You take the feathery ash upon your fingers.
You bring yourselves from the time past as it pleases you.

It is hard to return to the old nearness . . .

Harder to go again. . . .

THE VOICE OF THE ANNOUNCER

She is gone.
We know because the crowd is closing.
All we can see is the crowd closing.
We hear the releasing of held breath—
The weight shifting: the lifting of shoe leather.
The stillness is broken as surface of water is broken—
The sound circling from in outward.

(*The murmur of the crowd rises.*)

Small wonder they feel fear.
Before the murders of the famous kings—
Before imperial cities burned and fell—
The dead were said to show themselves and speak.

[8]

When dead men came disaster came. Presentiments
That let the living on their beds sleep on
Woke dead men out of death and gave them voices.
All ancient men in every nation knew this.

A VOICE OVER THE CROWD

Masterless men . . .

A VOICE OVER THE CROWD

When shall it be . . .

A VOICE OVER THE CROWD

Masterless men
Will take a master . . .

A VOICE OVER THE CROWD

What has she said to us . . .

A VOICE OVER THE CROWD

When shall it be . . .

A VOICE OVER THE CROWD

Masterless men
Will take a master.
Blood after . . .

A VOICE OVER THE CROWD

What has she said to us . . .

[9]

VOICES TOGETHER

Blood after!

*(The voices run together into the excited roar of
the crowd. The Announcer's voice is loud over it.)*

THE VOICE OF THE ANNOUNCER

They are milling around us like cattle that smell death.
The whole square is whirling and turning and shouting.
One of the ministers raises his arms on the platform.
No one is listening: now they are sounding drums:
Trying to quiet them likely: No! No!
Something is happening: there in the far corner:
A runner: a messenger: staggering: people are helping him:
People are calling: he comes through the crowd: they are
    quieter.
Only those on the far edge are still shouting:
Listen! He's here by the ministers now! He is speaking. . . .

THE VOICE OF THE MESSENGER

There has come the conqueror!
I am to tell you.
I have raced over sea land:
I have run over cane land:
I have climbed over cone land.
It was laid on my shoulders
By shall and by shan't
That standing by day
And staying by night

[10]

Were not for my lot
Till I came to the sight of you.
Now I have come.

Be warned of this conqueror!
This one is dangerous!
Word has out-oared him.
East over sea-cross has
All taken—
Every country.
No men are free there.
Ears overhear them.
Their words are their murderers.
Judged before judgment
Tried after trial
They die as do animals:—
Offer their throats
As the goat to her slaughterer.
Terror has taught them this!

Now he is here!

He was violent in his vessel:
He was steering in her stern:
He was watching in her waist:
He was peering in her prow:
And he dragged her up
Nine lengths
Till her keel lodged
On this nation.

Now he is here
Waylaying and night-lying.
If they hide before dark
He comes before sunup.
Where hunger is eaten
There he sits down:
Where fear sleeps
There he arises.

I tell you beware of him!
All doors are dangers.
The warders of wealth
Will admit him by stealth.
The lovers of men
Will invite him as friend.
The drinkers of blood
Will drum him in suddenly.
Hope will unlatch to him:
Hopelessness open.

I say and say truly
To all men in honesty
Such is this conqueror!
Shame is his people.
Lickers of spittle
Their lives are unspeakable:
Their dying indecent.

Be well warned!
He comes to you slightly
Slanting and sprinting

Hinting and shadowing:
Sly is his hiding:—
A hard lot:
A late rider:

Watch! I have said to you!

THE VOICE OF THE ANNOUNCER

They are leading him out: his legs give:
Now he is gone in the crowd: they are silent:
No one has spoken since his speaking:

They stand still circling the ministers.
No one has spoken or called out:—
There is no stir at all nor movement:
Even the farthest have stood patiently:
They wait trusting the old men:
They wait faithfully trusting the answer.
Now the huddle on the platform opens:
A minister turns to them raising his two arms. . . .

THE VOICE OF THE ORATOR

Freemen of this nation!
The persuasion of your wills against your wisdom is not
    dreamed of.
We offer themes for your consideration.

What is the surest defender of liberty?
Is it not liberty?

[13]

A free people resists by freedom:
Not locks! Not blockhouses!

The future is a mirror where the past
Marches to meet itself. Go armed toward arms!
Peaceful toward peace! Free and with music toward freedom!
Face tomorrow with knives and tomorrow's a knife-blade.
Murder your foe and your foe will be murder!—
Even your friends suspected of false-speaking:
Hands on the door at night and the floor boards squeaking.

Those who win by the spear are the spear-toters.
And what do they win? Spears! What else is there?
If their hands let go they have nothing to hold by.
They are no more free than a paralytic propped against a
    tree is.

With the armored man the arm is upheld by the weapon:
The man is worn by the knife.

Once depend on iron for your freedom and your
Freedom's iron!
Once overcome your resisters with force and your
Force will resist you!—
You will never be free of force.
Never of arms unarmed
Will the father return home:
The lover to her loved:
The mature man to his fruit orchard
Walking at peace in that beauty—
The years of his trees to assure him.

Force is a greater enemy than this conqueror—
A treacherous weapon.

Nevertheless my friends there *is* a weapon!
Weakness conquers!

Against chainlessness who breaks?
Against wall-lessness who vaults?
Against forcelessness who forces?

Against the feather of the thistle
Is blunted sharpest metal.
No edge cuts seed-fluff.

This conqueror unresisted
Will conquer no longer: a posturer
Beating his blows upon burdocks—
Shifting his guard against shadows.
Snickers will sound among road-menders:
Titters be stifled by laundresses:
Coarse guffaws among chambermaids.
Reddened with rage he will roar.
He will sweat in his uniform foolishly.
He will disappear: no one hear of him!

There *is* a weapon my friends.
Scorn conquers!

THE VOICE OF THE ANNOUNCER (*the Orator's voice
    unintelligible under it*)

I wish you could all see this as we do—
The whole plaza full of these people—

[15]

Their colorful garments—the harsh sunlight—
The water-sellers swinging enormous gourds—
The orator there on the stone platform—
The temple behind him: the high pyramid—
The hawks overhead in the sky teetering
Slow to the windward: swift to the down-wind—
The houses blind with the blank sun on them. . . .

THE VOICE OF THE ORATOR

There is a weapon.
Reason and truth are that weapon.

Let this conqueror come!
Show him no hindrance!
Suffer his flag and his drum!
Words . . . win!

THE VOICE OF THE ANNOUNCER

There's the shout now: he's done:
He's climbing down: a great speech:
They're all smiling and pressing around him:
The women are squatting in full sunlight:
They're opening packages: bread we'd say by the look—
Yes: bread: bread wrapped between corn leaves:
They're squatting to eat: they're quite contented and happy:
Women are calling their men from the sunny stones:
There are flutes sounding away off:
We can't see for the shifting and moving—
Yes: there are flutes in the cool shadow:
Children are dancing in intricate figures.

[16]

(*A drum and flute are
heard under the voice.*)

Even a few old men are dancing.
You'd say they'd never feared to see them dancing.
A great speech! really great!
Men forget these truths in passion:
They oppose the oppressors with blind blows:
They make of their towns tombs: of their roofs burials:
They build memorial ruins to liberty:
But liberty is not built from ruins:
Only in peace is the work excellent. . . .

That's odd! The music has stopped. There's something—
It's a man there on the far side: he's pointing:
He seems to be pointing back through the farthest street:
The people are twisting and rising: bread in their fists. . . .
We can't see what it is. . . . Wait! . . . it's a messenger.
It must be a messenger. Yes. It's a message—another.
Here he is at the turn of the street trotting:
His neck's back at the nape: he looks tired:
He winds through the crowd with his mouth open: laboring:
People are offering water: he pushes away from them:
Now he has come to the stone steps: to the ministers:
Stand by: we're edging in. . . .

(*There are sounds of people close by: coughs:
murmurs. The Announcer's voice is lowered.*)

Listen: he's leaning on the stone: he's speaking.

[17]

THE VOICE OF THE MESSENGER

There has come . . . the Conqueror. . . .

I am to tell you . . .

I have run over corn land:
I have climbed over cone land:
I have crossed over mountains. . . .

It was laid on my shoulders
By shall and by shan't
That standing by day
And staying by night
Were not for my lot
Till I came to the sight of you. . . .

Now I have come.

I bear word:
Beware of this conqueror!

The fame of his story
Like flame in the winter-grass
Widens before him.
Beached on our shore
With the dawn over shoulder
The lawns were still cold
When he came to the sheep meadows:—
Sun could not keep with him
So was he forward.

[18]

Fame is his sword.

No man opposing him
Still grows his glory.
He needs neither foeman nor
Thickset of blows to
Gather his victories—
Nor a foe's match
To earn him his battles.

He brings his own enemy!

He baggages with him
His closet antagonist—
His private opposer.
He's setting him up
At every road corner—
A figure of horror
With blood for his color:
Fist for his hand:
Reek where he stands:
Hate for his heat:
Sneers for his mouth:
Clouts for his clothes:
Oaths if he speak:—
And he's knocking him down
In every town square
Till hair's on his blade
And blood's all about
Like dust in a drouth
And the people are shouting

Flowers him flinging
Music him singing
And bringing him gold
And holding his heels
And feeling his thighs
Till their eyes start
And their hearts swell
And they're telling his praises
Like lays of the heroes
And chiefs of antiquity.

Such are his victories!
So does he come:
So he approaches. . . .

    (*A whisper rustles
    through the crowd.*)

No man to conquer
Yet as a conqueror
Marches he forward. . . .

    (*The whisper is louder.*)

Stands in your mountains. . . .

    (*A murmur of voices.*)

Soon to descend on you!

    (*A swelling roar.*)

THE VOICE OF THE ANNOUNCER

That touched them! That frightened them!
Some of them point to the east hills:
Some of them mock at the ministers: 'Freedom!'
'Freedom for what? To die in a rat trap?'
They're frantic with anger and plain fear.
They're sold out they say. You can hear them.
'Down with the government! Down with the orators!
'Down with liberal learned minds!
'Down with the mouths and the loose tongues in them!
'Down with the lazy lot! They've sold us!
'We're sold out! Talking has done for us!' . . .
They're boiling around us like mullet that smell shark.
We can't move for the mob: they're crazy with terror. . . .

A LOUD VOICE (*distant*)

God-lovers!
Think of your gods!

Earth-masters!
Taste your disasters!

Men!
Remember!

THE VOICE OF THE ANNOUNCER

There's a voice over the crowd somewhere.
They hear it: they're quieting down. . . . It's the priests!
We see them now: it's the priests on the pyramid!

[21]

There might be ten of them: black with their hair tangled.
The smoke of their fire is flat in the quick wind:
They stand in the thick of the smoke by the stone of the
    victims:
Their knives catch in the steep sun: they are shouting:
Listen!—

VOICES OF THE PRIESTS

Turn to your gods rememberers!

A SINGLE VOICE

Let the world be saved by surrendering the world:
    Not otherwise shall it be saved.

VOICES OF THE PRIESTS

Turn to your gods rememberers!

A SINGLE VOICE

Let evil be overcome by the coming over of evil:
    Your hearts shall be elsewhere.

VOICES OF THE PRIESTS

Turn to your gods rememberers!

VOICES OF THE PRIESTS (*antiphonally*)

Turn to your gods!
    The conqueror cannot take you!

[22]

Turn to your gods!
    The narrow dark will keep you!

Turn to your gods!
    In god's house is no breaking!

Turn to your gods!
    In god's silences sleep is!

Lay up your will with the gods!
    Stones cannot still you!

Lay up your mind with the gods!
    Blade cannot blind you!

Lay up your heart with the gods!
    Danger departs from you!

THE VOICE OF THE ANNOUNCER

It's a wonderful thing to see this crowd responding.
Even the simplest citizens feel the emotion.
There's hardly a sound now in the square. It's wonderful:
Really impressive: the priests there on the pyramid:
The smoke blowing: the bright sun: the faces—

A SINGLE VOICE

In the day of confusion of reason when all is delusion:
In the day of the tyrants of tongues when the truth is for hire:
In the day of deceit when ends meet:
Turn to your gods!

[23]

In the day of division of nations when hope is derision:
In the day of the supping of hate when the soul is corrupted:
In the day of despair when the heart's bare:
Turn to your gods!

(*A slow drum beat.*)

THE VOICE OF THE ANNOUNCER

A kind of dance is beginning: a serpent of people:
A current of people coiling and curling through people:
A circling of people through people like water through
    water. . . .

CHANTING VOICES (*to the drums*)

Out of the stir of the sun
Out of the shout of the thunder
Out of the hush of the star . . .
Withdraw the heart.

THE VOICE OF THE ANNOUNCER (*the chant and drums under*)

A very young girl is leading them:
They have torn the shawl from her bare breast:
They are giving her flowers: her mouth laughs:
Her eyes are not laughing. . . .

CHANTING VOICES

Leave now the lovely air
To the sword and the sword-wearer—

[24]

Leave to the marksman the mark—
Withdraw the heart.

THE VOICE OF THE ANNOUNCER (*the chant and drums louder*)

She's coming . . . the drums pound . . . the crowd
Shrieks . . . she's reaching the temple . . . she's climbing
    it. . . .
Others are following: five: ten . . .
Hundreds are following . . . crowding the stairway. . . .
She's almost there . . . her flowers have fallen . . .
She looks back . . . the priests are surrounding her. . . .

  (*The drums suddenly stop: there is an instant's
  silence: then an angry shout from the crowd.*)

THE VOICE OF THE ANNOUNCER

Wait! Wait! Something has happened!
One of the ministers: one of the oldest:
The general: the one in the feathered coat:—
He's driving them down with the staff of a banner:
He's climbed after them driving them down:
There's shouting and yelling enough but they're going:
He's telling them off too: you can hear him—

A DEEP VOICE (*chatter of the crowd under it*)

Men! Old men! Listen!
Twist your necks on your nape bones!
The knife will wait in the fist for you.

There is a time for everything—
Time to be thinking of heaven:
Time of your own skins!

Cock your eyes to the windward!

Do you see smoke on those mountains?
The smoke is the smoke of towns.
And who makes it? The conqueror!
And where will he march now? Onward!
The heel of the future descends on you!

THE VOICE OF THE ANNOUNCER

He has them now: even the priests have seen it:
They're all looking away here to the east.
There's smoke too: filling the valleys: like thunderheads! . . .

THE VOICE OF THE GENERAL

You are foolish old men.

You ought to be flogged for your foolishness.
Your grandfathers died to be free
And you—you juggle with freedom!
Do you think you're free by a law
Like the falling of apples in autumn?

You thought you were safe in your liberties!
You thought you could always quibble!
You can't! You take my word for it.
Freedom's the rarest bird!

[26]

You risk your neck to snare it—
It's gone while your eyeballs stare!

Those who'd lodge with a tyrant
Thinking to feed at his fire
And leave him again when they're fed are
Plain fools or were bred to it—
Brood of the servile races
Born with the hang-dog face. . . .

THE VOICE OF THE ANNOUNCER

They're all pointing and pushing together:
The women are shouldering baskets: bread: children. . . .
They smell smoke in the air: they smell terror. . . .

THE VOICE OF THE GENERAL (*louder over the increasing
    sound*)

There's nothing in this world worse—
Empty belly or purse or the
Pitiful hunger of children—
Than doing the Strong Man's will!

The free will fight for their freedom.
They're free men first. They feed
Meager or fat but as free men.
Everything else comes after—
Food: roof: craft—
Even the sky and the light of it!

[27]

(*The voices of the crowd rise to a tumult of sounds—drums: shouts: cries.*)

THE VOICE OF THE ANNOUNCER

The sun is yellow with smoke . . . the town's burning. . . .
The war's at the broken bridge. . . .

THE VOICE OF THE GENERAL (*shouting*)

You! Are you free? Will you fight?

There are still inches for fighting!

There is still a niche in the streets!

You can stand on the stairs and meet him!

You can hold in the dark of a hall!

You can die!

—or your children will crawl for it!

THE VOICE OF THE ANNOUNCER (*over the tumult*)

They won't listen. They're shouting and screaming and circling.
The square is full of deserters with more coming.
Every street from the bridge is full of deserters.
They're rolling in with the smoke blowing behind them.
The plaza's choked with the smoke and the struggling of
stragglers.

[28]

They're climbing the platform: driving the ministers: shout-
　　ing—
One speaks and another:

THE VOICES OF CITIZENS

The city is doomed!
　　　　　　　　There's no holding it!

Let the conqueror have it! It's his!

The age is his! It's his century!

Our institutions are obsolete.
He marches a mile while we sit in a meeting.

Opinions and talk!
Deliberative walks beneath the ivy and the creepers!

The age demands a made-up mind.
The conqueror's mind is decided on everything.

His doubt comes after the deed or never.

He knows what he wants for his want's what he knows.
He's gone before they say he's going.
He's come before you've barred your house.

He's one man: we are but thousands!

Who can defend us from one man?

Bury your arms! Break your standards!

Give him the town while the town stands!

THE VOICE OF THE ANNOUNCER

They're throwing their arms away: their bows are in bonfires.
The plaza is littered with torn plumes: spear-handles. . . .

THE VOICES OF CITIZENS

Masterless men! . . .

Masterless men
Must take a master! . . .

Order must master us! . . .

Freedom's for fools:
Force is the certainty!

Freedom has eaten our strength and corrupted our virtues!

Men must be ruled!

Fools must be mastered!

Rigor and fast
Will restore us our dignity!

Chains will be liberty!

THE VOICE OF THE ANNOUNCER

The last defenders are coming: they whirl from the streets like
Wild leaves on a wind: the square scatters them.

[30]

Now they are fewer—ten together or five:
They come with their heads turned: their eyes back.

Now there are none. The street's empty—in shadow.
The crowd is retreating—watching the empty street:
The shouts die.

   The voices are silent.

       They're watching. . . .

They stand in the slant of the sunlight silent and watching.
The silence after the drums echoes the drum beat.

Now there's a sound. They see him. They must see him!
They're shading their eyes from the sun: there's a rustle of
  whispering:
We can't see for the glare of it. . . . Yes! . . . Yes! . . .
He's there in the end of the street in the shadow. We see him!
He looks huge—a head taller than anyone:
Broad as a brass door: a hard hero:
Heavy of heel on the brick: clanking with metal:
The helm closed on his head: the eyeholes hollow.

He's coming! . . .
    He's clear of the shadow! . . .
       The sun takes him.

They cover their faces with fingers. They cower before him.
They fall: they sprawl on the stone. He's alone where he's
  walking.
He marches with rattle of metal. He tramples his shadow.

He mounts by the pyramid—stamps on the stairway—turns—
His arm rises—his visor is opening. . . .

    (*There is an instant's breathless silence: then the*
voice of the Announcer low—almost a whisper.)

                                          There's no one! . . .
There's no one at all! . . .
                    No one! . . .
                              The helmet is hollow!
The metal is empty! The armor is empty! I tell you
There's no one at all there: there's only the metal:
The barrel of metal: the bundle of armor. It's empty!

The push of a stiff pole at the nipple would topple it.

They don't see! They lie on the paving. They lie in the
Burnt spears: the ashes of arrows. They lie there . . .
They don't see or they won't see. They are silent. . . .

The people invent their oppressors: they wish to believe in
    them.
They wish to be free of their freedom: released from their
    liberty:—
The long labor of liberty ended!
                            They lie there!

    (*There is a whisper of sound.*
    The Announcer's voice is louder.)

Look! It's his arm! It is rising! His arm's rising!
They're watching his arm as it rises. They stir. They cry.

They cry out. They are shouting. They're shouting with happiness.

Listen! They're shouting like troops in a victory. Listen—
'The city of masterless men has found a master!'
You'd say it was they were the conquerors: they that had conquered.

A ROAR OF VOICES

The city of masterless men has found a master!
The city has fallen!
The city has fallen!

THE VOICE OF THE ANNOUNCER (*flat*)

The city has fallen. . . .

[33]